"This book is profoundly beautiful, challenging, disturbing, and a must read . . . the words are powerful, raw, tender, engaging, and I wanted more. That is how I judge a really good book – does it leave me wanting more."

> -- Esther Armstrong, Writer, Lecturer,
>
> Portland, Oregon

"The first page captured my attention, so I read it all. It did much to help me begin to understand the helplessness that some feel. I firmly believe that real ministry happens when we care for those who are down and can be a part of their regaining hope.

> --David Petty, Building Contractor,
>
> Clovis, New Mexico

"I enjoyed your book – it's all too familiar. I'm going to share your book with several others here at FCI Texarkana. Had two men today ask if they could read it."

> ■ Rickey, FCI   Texarkana, Texas

"What courage, strength, and hope!! I cannot bear to part with my copy. I will need many more in the future."

> -- Dianne Hunter, State Director FAMM,
>
> Edmond, Oklahoma

1

How to Strive, Thrive and Stay Alive in Prison

A

Kenneth Shelby Armstrong Th.D., Ed.D.

KennethWrites@me.com

Contents

Part 1

How to Strive

When you go into prison, **Striving** is the hard part. You have just gone through the terrible ordeals of investigation, indictment, trial, and sentencing. If that's not enough to destroy you, you are a rare breed. By the time you get processed by the prison you will have been thoroughly demeaned, humiliated, and de-humanized. The whole process is horrible. It shouldn't happen to a cat.

There is a sentence in a popular song that says, "Pick yourself up. Brush yourself off. And start all over again." What they are saying is—Strive!

It makes no difference if you were guilty or not. You have been classified as being the worst of the worst. If that doesn't destroy your self-image, nothing will. You have probably never been this far down, and you probably will never again go through this kind of punishment.

In spite of how you are feeling,

Just, "Pick yourself up. Brush yourself off. And start all over again." Strive!

We, as a society, are just becoming aware of the fact that a large percentage of those in prison were not guilty at all. They just had incompetent and uncaring attorneys representing them. Money is a big problem. Most **inside** did not have the financial resources to defend themselves, so in reality the poor get the worst punishment. They had to just accept whatever was dealt out to them. Unfair? Yes! Deplorable? Yes!

But, "Pick yourself up. Brush yourself off. And start all over again." Strive!

The word STRIVE is not a common word that we use everyday, but it is a powerful word. The dictionary defines it as:

"Making great effort to achieve or obtain something valuable."

"To struggle vigorously towards a goal."

It means to go all out, to fight, to work hard, to advance, make progress.

And the opposite of STRIVING is to fail, decline, wither.

Some inmates go *inside* and collapse. They give up and go into some sort of isolated hibernation. They feel sorry for themselves. They spend all their time playing cards or watching TV. They lose the use of the time that has been given to them. They come out worse off than when they went in.

Others give into bitterness, and take out their misery and hostility on others. They go down to the yard and lift weights and exercise. They spend their time on their bodies and forget that their brains are atrophying. They come out worse off than when they went in.

Everyone looks for some way of coping with their problems, but few see that their problems do not have to be as bad as they think them to be. Actually, their problems are hiding something of great value.

They don't see that their problems are hiding some great opportunities. They have been given time to plan and prepare their futures. They have been given time to prepare for a great tomorrow.

When I went *inside* I was already 70 years old. Immediately *fear* grabbed me by the throat and told me that my life was over. I was told that I could never get a job at my age when I got out. I was reminded that I did not have any money, and there was no way of getting any.

Fear convinced me that I had one huge problem and it was **BIG**. I had spent all the money that we had on lawyers. I had no one to help me. It was my problem and I had to take care of my wife as well as myself. Impossible!

I thought perhaps I could get a job teaching. I had four graduate degrees including two doctorates, but who would want to hire a 70 year old ex-con. I crossed that off my list.

I thought about building houses, But I had no money and at my age that wouldn't be a solution that would be viable over a long stretch of time. **FEAR** vexed me every day and wouldn't let me sleep at night. What could I do?

A small glimmer of hope entered my mind one day. It was a long-shot, but it just might work. I thought that I might be able to write some stories about events and people that I had known, and sell them. The problem was that I didn't know how to write that kind of work. I knew how to write academic theses and dissertations, but that was a hundred miles from writing things that people would enjoy.

But my options were few and I decided to give it a try. I remembered a story that they told me in Africa when I lived there.

They said that a man was out in the grasslands being chased by a rogue elephant. He looked for a tree to climb, but there were none anywhere close. Finally, he saw a lone tree about a half a mile away. He said to himself, "I could never outrun that elephant to that tree." But since he had no other option he said, "Well, I might as well try. I don't have any other option."

So he ran and sure enough he beat the elephant to the tree, but when he got there he saw that the lowest limb was 15 feet off the ground. He told himself that he could never jump that high. It was impossible, but he said "I might as well try. I have no other options."

So he jumped with all his strength. His friend asked if he had caught it. He replied, "No, but I caught it on my way down."

When your options are few, *TRY,* anyway. That is what **striving** is all about.

My glimmer of hope seemed almost impossible, but I decided to give it a try. I started writing stories and poems. They weren't very good, but it was a start. I encouraged myself by thinking that perhaps before my time was up i would be able to write well enough to sell a story and make enough to stay alive. So I wrote. I wrote every day.

One day I met an inmate who seemed to be a very civilized and agreeable sort of fellow. We got to talking and I found out that he had been given a sentence that would mean that he would be a very old man when he got out. He had been accused of being the major drug distributor in the State of Alaska.

That accusation didn't seem to fit him at all. He was refined and very well versed in literature. I told him that I was trying to learn to write and he immediately said that I should read a book on writing that he had read. The author was Jon Franklin and the title was **Writing For Story**. The writer had won two Pulitzer prizes and was a professor of writing.

I ordered the book immediately, and when I read it, it blew me away. I had never read anything like it. Wow! I decided to let that book be my professor. I started re-reading the book.

I soon found that my largest task was that of **unlearning** what I had taken decades to learn. I assumed that all that I had learned in my academic writing would make the writing process automatic. It was not automatic. It was the most difficult thing that I had ever attempted.

But, I kept trying to learn how to write something that the average person would enjoy reading. I had hundreds of stories all around me. I was in prison and every prisoner had at least one good story to tell.

So I determined to write my stories and put them into a book. Although the book was mostly based in the prison system, I thought that perhaps the book would sell and then I could write another book. It was not my intention to start a revolution or castigate those who operate the criminal justice system, neither did I wish to develop an apology for those incarcerated in that system.

When I started writing, I posted a note before me to keep me focused on what I was trying to accomplish. That note read:

"This is a book about how it *feels* to be:

accused, investigated, committed, alienated,

punished, stigmatized, separated, abused,

demeaned, and virtually enslaved."

The point of this part of my journey was to show that I strived. I tried to think about the future and to be excited about it. I read every book on writing that I could find and I practiced writing every day.

And the truth is that everyone can strive. Striving doesn't have to be about writing. It can be about preparing to learn and enter some profession, or building some small business, or learning a trade, or earning a degree in some subject that captures your imagination. But it is about working hard once you have found your goal.

Forget the past with all of its problems. Just "Pick yourself up. Brush yourself off. And start all over again." Strive!

And now at this point let me offer you a few stories and poems that I wrote in prison. Read them and give me a grade for my work. I do hope that they can help both you and someone that you know who is in prison. I received this note from an inmate in Texas who had read this book.

"I enjoyed your book—it's all too familiar. I'm going to share your book with several others here at FCI Texarkana. Had two men today ask if they could read it."

■ Rickey, FCI, Texarkana, Texas

Regret

My cellie was a former boxing champion. He had been a golden glover in the State of Oklahoma. He enjoyed taking the boxing stance and dance around the the pod, and punch some imaginary foe. I could not, but I am sure he could hear the roar of the crowd as he stalked the illusive champion.

He had pictures, too. He carried them in his wallet, and he showed them to anyone who displayed the slightest interest. The pictures were more valuable to him than a bank account back home. I enjoyed his boxing stories. He was sure that he could have reached the big time, if he had not hurt his hand, and he protected it as if it were the most important thing of his body.

Once or twice his enthusiasm got the better of his good sense, and he pounded another inmate, with lightning quickness and savage power. I was sure that his quick temper would get him in trouble, but he was fortunate. He never reached the hole.

One day I went to my room and found him there, sobbing into his hands. A letter lay on the table, and I knew that the news in it was not good. I went to my bunk and tried to act as if nothing was amiss.

"When I saw that his emotion was ebbing, I asked, "Can I do anything?"

"There's nothing anyone can do. It has been done already. I'm the guy to blame. Now it's too late."

"Nothing is ever too late," I said.

"Oh yes it is. It's too late to be there when my boys need me. Sammy is only 16, and they've arrested him and put him in jail, just like his father—me—and I'm not there to help him when he needs me most. By the time I get out of prison, both of my kids will probably be in prison. What a fool I am, and I'm not only paying the price for my stupidity, so are my boys."

He cried again—heaving great sobs. His remorse quieted eventually, but then it turned into anger. He was angry with himself. He was angry with the people who were keeping him from his family. He left the room to go find someone to vent his frustration on.

I knew how he felt. I had my own valise of regrets, and I knew that if regrets were buffaloes, we would be living in the middle of a stampede. Prison was kind enough to give everyone time enough to find regret.

When all else failed to give comfort, I found that I could crawl into a quiet corner of my soul and write a poem. I discovered that words did have the power to bring peace, no matter how deep the hurt. I wrote…

Turn your back on dark regret.
There's no treasure to be found.
Ashes, dust, and broken dreams,
life's trash, piled high around.

Turn your back on tear-filled nights.
Contemplation yields no rest.
Failures, errors, disappointments
are no food for this day's test.

Turn your back on all your sorrow.
You will find no nourishment.
Broken friendships, gone forever,
are no fount of encouragement.

Now, turn your face to greet the sun.
Let all your shadows fall behind.
Darkness flees in view of light.
Tomorrow's providence will be kind.

For all you need is one good friend,
one vowed and tried as true.
And when you need someone who cares,
this friend is there for you.

Cry and Say Goodbye

My adventure began at the federal transfer center in Oklahoma City. I was informed that this would be my home for the first two years of my sentence. I was immediately assigned to be a tutor in the prison's GED program.

This was to be one of the richest experiences of my life and one of the most painful. One of my students was a young Mexican boy. He was in his late twenties, bright, but uneducated. In the first five minutes of the class, he grasped the concept the teacher proposed, and then promptly went to sleep. He never did any assigned homework. He brought his body to class, parked it in sleep, and then his mind flew off to some distant place. It was the best way to serve fifteen years behind bars, or so it seemed to him. He, like a few others, still had an intact family, and he wanted to be home with his wife and children. So he dreamed.

Every afternoon for exercise I walked the aisles of our triangular pod. I usually chose a time for my walking when everyone was eating a meal, or taking early evening naps. It was the best I could do for exercise, for we were never permitted to go outside and walk on the dirt or grass. We were like industrial chickens, living entirely in a penned environment.

As I walked one day, I noticed my young Mexican student on the phone. The large room was empty except for two or three of us. I heard him laughing as he talked on the phone to someone obviously dear to him. Then suddenly he quit laughing and yelled out, "Ohhhhhh noooooooo!"

Then he slammed the receiver down and ran up the steps to his cell. We passed each other on the walkway, but he kept his head lowered and did not look at me. I heard his door slam, but did not look around. I continued my walk.

On my next round, as I passed his door, I listened for any noise inside. I thought that he might be crying, but I heard nothing. I continued my walking. When I came to his door again all was quiet, but as I walked on, I heard a noise—a bump on the door. I walked back and heard it again. I knocked on his door and yelled, "Are you okay?" There was no response. I tried the knob, but it would not turn. I looked around and saw a correctional officer enter the pod and walk toward his desk. "Mr. Johnson," I yelled. "You'd better come up here. Something's wrong."

In measured, but not hurried strides, Johnson mounted the steps and came to the door. He tried the knob, but it would not turn. He tried again, harder, and it turned. He jerked the door open, and there, two legs dangled squarely in the center of the opening. The boy's feet were still swinging, bumping the doorjamb, as his life twitched away.

Johnson grabbed the boy's legs and tried to take the weight off the sheet tied around his neck. Another inmate rushed up to help the struggling guard. But it took too long to get his body down. Johnson bent over the lifeless body for several minutes administering artificial resuscitation. The young man did not respond. Finally, Johnson said, "He's dead." They brought a stretcher and placed his body on it. Four inmates carried him down the stairs toward the door.

Sleep was not a friend that night. I used the night's vacant hours to mourn, to pray, and to consider the harshness of life. In memory of my friend, I wrote a poem. It was not much, but it was the least I could do for him.

The sun came up, and the new day forgot the pain of the last. It is always that way in prison. Pain is transient. There is no need to hold onto it; the supply is endless.

Warning bells don't always ring
when danger comes our way.
Skies can be blue, and birds can sing

on each man's final day.

Roaring winds don't always blow
a signal to a gale.
Our closest friends don't always know
our hearts are faint and quail.

We do not know that moment when
resolve to live is dead.
Our minds and hearts can seldom ken,
that time when hope has fled.

The death of love, the broken pledge,
is more than some can bear.
Death invites. They walk the ledge,
the path of bleak despair.

Oh, that I could call you back;
new life to you apply.
That miracle is power I lack;
I cry, and say, goodbye.

Chained Grace

My prison was a model of electronic and computerized security. Millions of dollars were spent to make it escape-proof and impenetrable. Each night, it stands bathed in light as sophisticated cameras sweep the building, the grounds, and the streets for any threat of entry.

Giant steel cables embedded in hidden trenches protect the perimeter of the building. Should a terrorist load a truck with explosives and propel it toward this facility, the cables will spring from their hiding and stop any mechanical giant. It is impregnable. It is my home.

Yet each night, when the guards relax, and the prisoners settle down for another night of sleep, he finds a way in. The monitored halls, the steel doors, are not impediments. He stalks to my bunk. He pushes me from sleep. I know him. His name isTerror.

He is no stranger to me. For months before I entered the transfer center, he had visited my home. Late at night he came and stayed long hours. His message was always the same.

Sure, you can make it in prison, but what about your wife? She'll never survive. They'll tear her apart. She'll be like a baby in a den of wolves. You'll probably never see her again. You can't even imagine what it's like in there. I had to agree with him. She was not equipped to handle hard women and a harsh environment

Terror dipped his hands into my brain and played with my thoughts. He struck my nerves and beat them like strings on a banjo. His music was not a song; it was a scream, and I choked on it. At dawn he left my cell, but not before he bathed me in my own sweat as fear seeped into my pores. I could smell it all day long.

In the beginning the prison would not let me call her. They would not let me write her. I was not permitted to receive the smallest scrap of reassurance from her. My imagination had been captured by terror and it served me poorly.

The prison regimen kept me busy during the days, which was good. I had no time to think about the problems that plagued me at night. I liked my work, and I liked those for whom I worked. I wondered why my wife couldn't have been treated as kindly as I.

My supervisor came for me one morning to take me to my work station. We entered the elevator to go down to level two. The elevator stopped. The doors opened and we exited.

Coming across the lobby toward us was a beautiful woman, perhaps in her mid-thirties. She wore the plain dress of an inmate, and as she came, it seemed as if she were dancing, gliding to music no one else could hear. She smiled as she passed, and then I noticed two guards following her. I stopped and turned back to see her again. She stood there, facing the elevator, with her hands behind her back— handcuffed. The elevator door opened. She stepped inside and turned around as her guards pushed past her. She was smiling as the doors closed.

Late that night I saw her again in my memory. I saw the handcuffs. I saw the guards. I saw the smile. I didn't know who the girl was, but I thought, perhaps she was there to show me that my wife, though under guard, was somewhere wearing a smile, as well.

I tried to sleep, but my brain buzzed with words. I found myself repeating phrases and sentences that I did not want to lose. I groped for pencil and paper, and although I could not see, I scrawled the words on paper, hoping I could read them in the morning.

Throughout the night, other phrases pushed me awake and I scrawled them on fresh pieces of paper. When dawn came, I took the papers and deciphered the scrawls. I knew the words were not about the girl, but about my wife. Somewhere she was smiling—smiling, not that her circumstances were pleasant, but that she had found a secret and she would survive. I knew she would survive and win. There was strength in her softness that terror had not shown me.

There she stands in slender grace.

Chains — on her wrists.

A smile — on her face.

There's no protest, no frown of hate.

Surrendered — at last.

At peace — with fate.

Kindness birthed not that rueful smile.

Contented — her lot.

Judged — no guile.

A smile? What secret had she found?

Forgiveness — from above?

Contentment — though bound?

There she stands in beauteous grace.

A thorn in her heart.

A rose on her face.

Part 2

How to Thrive

The good news is that if you Strive, you will Thrive. That truth comes out of a scripture that says what so ever a person sows, that shall they also reap. And, of course if you sow in abundance, you will reap in abundance.

"Thriving means to get ahead, to prosper, to advance, to do well.

And the opposite of STRIVING is failing, declineing, withering, losing ground.

Thriving is not an automatic process to living. Just because you are alive and have a good job, does not mean you are thriving. Thriving involves abundance. It generally means going the extra mile. Doing and enjoying more than that of the average person means you are thriving.

The tools that are necessary for thriving are obtainable. Not all people have them and not all people who do have them, use them.

Education is a great and almost necessary tool. It is important to choose the type of education that you need. Fortunately, you live in a time where the possibilities of education are almost limitless. Do some research before you start your educational journey. If you must get your educational program after a day's work—do it anyway. it will pay big dividends. Get good advice on your selection. Go to the smartest person that you know and ask for help. They will give it to you.

Experience is a great tool. Try more than one thing before you put all your eggs in one basket. If you have to start out at the bottom, make sure that the person you work for can give you the experience that you will need.

Failure is a great tool. Don't be afraid to fail. Most people learn more by failing than they do by succeeding. Don't be rash, but be brave. Don't let failure prohibit you from trying again.

Relationships can be a great tool. If you know someone who has the ability to help you, cultivate that relationship. Be honest with him or her.

Habits are great tools. Punctuality is a great tool. Always be on time. It will pay off with great benefit to you in all matters of your life and work. And, of course, bad habits can/will destroy your future. Get rid of all your bad habits as soon as possible. It pays off.

Reading and Writing are tremendous tools.Set up a good reading program and stick to it. Learn to write a good sentence. I started a program of reading when I was young. I kept a reading pile where I put everything that I thought I should read. When the pile got too high, I quit everything to get the pile reduced.

I get up every morning at about 3:00 and read until 7:00. I have been doing this for decades. My Dad followed that pattern also. I remember my father telling me that if you don't put things into your brain, you will scarcely be able to get much out of your brain. I can't forget that statement. It is too true.

Diminish television to as few hours as you can. Watching television is like eating sawdust for breakfast.

Eddie Cantor, the famous comedian once said, "If we keep watching television the way we are now, we will soon breed a race with eyes the size of saucers and brains the size of peas."

Another thing about writing is that you must spend more time **thinking** than you do writing. Many people just don't think. They live by instinct, hunch, or habit. To be successful you must be a thinker. Here are some stories and poems that have come about through thought.

Everyone Needs an Angel

The room was as dark as Satan's soul. My awakening eyes searched for any hint of light, form, or shadow. Nothing! This was my bedroom, but it felt like a tomb. What was wrong? I groped for my wife's familiar form, but there was only her perfume, where her body should have been. I moved to the bedroom door, opened it, and listened. The sounds of weeping and muffled sobs coming from the living room found my ears, and it cut to my heart.

"Babe?" I ventured. "Are you okay?"

"I'm fine. Go back to bed. I'll be there in a few minutes. Right now I need to be alone."

I turned and reentered the blackness. I had not asked her what was wrong, because I knew already and there was nothing I could do to fix it. That afternoon we had stood in a federal courtroom and learned that in sixty days we would both be entering separate prisons.

We had made the three-hour trip home a trail of tears. The evening had gone by slowly as the reality of prison sank deeper into the pits of our stomachs. I hoped that nightfall would erase the ominous reality of the day, but it did not. She never returned to bed, and I never returned to sleep.

The sixty days crawled by slowly, and there was too much time for black anticipation. But, at the same time, the sixty days sped by rapidly, and there was too little time to prepare our affairs for a four-year absence.

Time was not a smooth, straight string. It was gnarled yarn. During the days I worked in an anxious fever to get everything done. At night, I fought the giant demons of fear.

For my wife's sake I held it together, but inside, my thoughts were running at a frantic pace. My wife stayed by my side, but she suffered at each step. I was suffering too, both for her and for our shattered lives, but I hoped it didn't show. Her anxious dialogue was a volcano of questions. I had few answers, and those I offered were light, like ashes, and quickly blew away.

Finally, on January 3rd, we were both incarcerated in federal prisons. She went to one in Fort Worth, Texas, and I went to one in Oklahoma City. Neither of us knew what to expect, but we knew whatever it was, it would last a long time. Four years may not seem like such a long time, but it is if you are away from the one you love. I once opined that all of life is what you make it, but I discovered that it's hard to make diamonds out of mud.

A thousand days of writing letters passed, and I wrote her, "I wouldn't have missed this experience for anything in the world. Talk about adventure, this has been the greatest!"

In her next letter she replied, "Yes, I agree with you. I'm glad we came to prison. But even though I wouldn't trade anything for the time I've spent in here, once is enough. Let's not sign up for another term!"

I asked her how she had survived the ordeal. She wrote back, "Two things helped me through the rough spots. One was the scripture that you reminded me of, and the other was the poem that you wrote for me. They were lifesavers."

"No disaster shall befall you, no calamity shall come upon your home. For he has charged his angels to guard you wherever you go..." Psalms 91:10.

Everyone needs an angel,
for life is lonely, cold, unkind;
and crying out does no one good,
the fears like bees swarm the mind.

Everyone needs an angel.
The path winds down into the flood,
and friends like stars hide themselves;
the moon and hope turn to blood.

Everyone needs an angel,
for condemnation burns inside.
We have no balm to soothe or heal
the guilt that lives, but which we hide.

But a stranger smiled.

    A child laughed loud.

        A red bird sang.

            A tree waved proud.

A flower bloomed.

    The wind caressed.

        And I saw the reason

            why I'm so blest.

                God gave me an angel!

YOU!

The Patriot

I am convinced that the worst job in the entire federal prison system is in the wash room of the transfer center in Oklahoma City. The kitchen at the transfer center has the responsibility of preparing as many as 4,000 meals each day, which means that someone must empty 4,000 trays, 4,000 cups, 4,000 plates, and 4,000 of any other item used to feed the transient prisoners.

The prisoners who were assigned to the wash room received all these items, banged them against large sinks to remove most of the remaining food, and then washed them with hot water and steam. The noise in that small room was deafening. The smell was nauseous. The heat was stifling. The maximum punishment for any inmate was to be sent to the wash room.

The inmate dining area was located only a few feet from the wash room. It was almost impossible to carry on a conversation with a friend across the table from you because of the noise. I dreaded meal time. Most inmates went into the area, ate their meals, and got out as soon as possible.

George Trent was assigned to the wash room permanently. He was a striking figure. He was at least six foot six inches tall. He had a barrel chest that looked like iron. His shoulders were wide, and when he stood up he looked like a giant armored warrior. But, there was no surrender in his countenance, and the prison offered him no respite. He was there when I arrived, and he was still there when I left. He was given a special brand of punishment, for he was a special kind of inmate.

George slipped into the chair across from where I was eating. "You're new here, aren't you? Are you from Texas?"

"Yes, I'm new, and no, I'm not from Texas. Why do you ask if I'm from Texas?"

"Well Texas is my home and it's in a lot of trouble. I was hopeing that I could get a new recruit for the Republic of Texas."

"What's the Republic of Texas? I thought it was the State of Texas."

"No sir, it's the Republic of Texas, and I'm one of its patriots. Do you mean you haven't heard of the movement to get Texas back into the hands of its own citizens? Why man, we're about to get our independence back. We have elected all our republic officers. We have our own currency and everything. The feds don't like it, and they're coming down on us. That's why I have permanent duty in that hole in there. They're trying to break me, but they'll never do it."

"You already have your independence. Why are you fighting the government?"

"The founders of Texas never expected things to turn out the way it has. They never did want Washington to run Texas the way it does. The feds perpetuated a fraud on the citizens of Texas, and now we are slaves of a foreign government. Real Texans don't like that."

The next time I met George was in chapel. He was a consistent attendant. He brought his well-read bible, and sang louder than anyone else. At times I saw him crying and praying for strength to remain steadfast in his calling. He loved the old hymns. He hardly ever stopped smiling.

I did not understand his cause, but I admired his strength and conviction. I wrote a poem about him and when I read it to him, he broke into tears and asked me to please send a copy of it to his wife. He said that she did not understand the war that he was fighting. She didn't know why he was in prison. George thought the poem might help her. I sent it to her.

Tall, he stands and resolute.
No shifting eyes. No compromise.
Tall, like an oak, with uncommon strength,
and power to see the unseen prize.

'Twas principle that brought him down
to count the hours and waste the years.
'Tis principle that lifts him high
to conquer human midnight fears.

Had he been born a yore ago,
he would've been a king, or some grand thing.
But here in this bleak time and place,
he's a muffled bird with broken wing.

Another century and a different scene —
his voice would have been a song.
But when man forgets sweet liberty,
what has been right can turn to wrong.

Tall, he stands, unmoved by shame.
He cares not for the odds.
He cannot win. He will not lose.
The battle's not his, but God's.

A Poem for Us

The drudge of prison cannot be understood by those on the outside. Inside, drudgery becomes the norm, and men accommodate to living for years like cattle in a feed lot. Feelings soon dissolve. Numbness is the plague. Banality is its brother. No genius of imagination can capture the feelings produced by repetitious food, monotonous clothing, tedious work, and the same, same, bland faces.

One of my duties in prison was to dust the beautiful books that lay quietly, undisturbed in the special bookcase in my supervisor's office. These were not the usual books provided to the inmates. Inmates prefer Capone, Scarface, and the classic, The Texas Chainsaw Murders. I enjoyed dusting the beautiful books with the gilded bindings. And then I found it – 100 Greatest Poems. What a discovery! Imagine, 100 Greatest Poems in this hell of a place.

"Mrs. Hammond," I ventured. "I want to teach a course in poetry appreciation."

"Poetry, in here?" She looked surprised.

"Yes. Men in here have souls, even if they've forgotten it. Poetry can help them come alive and find themselves."

"Mr.Armstrong, get me a course outline and a resource guide, and if you can find six inmates who will enroll, you can have your class."

I found them—exactly six, and what a menagerie! The banker was first to enroll. I knew he would. He was a sensitive, kind, good person. My second student was a crafty little guy who dreamed of becoming a writer. The fact that he had little schooling did not deter him. He burned to write the sequel to The Texas Chainsaw Murders. I expected he would, too. My third student was a fifty year old biker, still living in the sixties. Having run out of space on his body for tattoos, he ate incessantly, pushing his belly out into a new expanse for more art.

A quiet little Mexican man enrolled and would have made an excellent student had he been able to understand English. He could not, although he tried to hide it. A man accused of child pornography joined the class in a fruitless attempt to be accepted by any group inside prison. And then there was DeeDee – the gay.

"That's quite a class you have there, Mr. Armstrong," Mrs. Hammond said with a bemused smile. "Go with it, and good luck."

It was not just good luck that came to us in that class. The words of the masters flowed over us like maple syrup over pancakes, and it was sweet, satisfying, and a warm ritual of shared emotion. The taste of it came to us, one by one, and a change began to occur in their eyes. And then we were different, changed by the words that came streaming from the past and washing over us.

Poetry narrowed the distance between us. The great poems were playgrounds where we met and played in innocence without the baggage of adulthood. This is rare in prison. Prison is a place where bodies are close, but where miles must be covered to reach your nearest neighbor.

Prison is a lonely landscape. You see people on the horizon, but you never get close enough to know much about them. Poetry changed that for us. We became a community. When the class was over, I wrote a poem for all of us.

A poem is like a newborn babe,
all wrinkled and ugly and red.
It's nothing but a lump of words,
not living, but yet not dead.

A babe must grow and suffer a lot,
and build muscle and sinew and flesh.
A poem must throb and find its own life,
inspired by a dream that's fresh.

First bred, it speaks not ever a word,
no beauty is there to enjoy.
But nourish it often to your breast,
it brings thought and abundant joy.

Poems are not written in mansions fair,
or places of luxury.
They are written in cells of secret pain,
deep pools of misery.

Not written are they to increase the pain,
but to yield the pain to thought.
For in each pain, there can be gain,
and victory can be bought.

A poem is like a man grown tall
and strong of back and mind.
It's weathered the storms of fear and doubt.
It lives to bless mankind.

Polarity

I had never known or talked to a homosexual before, at least not to my knowledge. To me, these were mysterious creatures encroaching the outer boundaries of civility and morality, usually repulsed by noble citizens. I did not realize that they had hearts, brains, and guts that writhed in the night. I did not care to know more than what I presumed.

But DeeDee made that impossible. She had tasted the nectar of poetry and she thirsted for more. There! It slipped out—that word *she*. I discovered that I and others used *she* more often than he when referring to DeeDee.

I once apologized for the slip of the tongue, but she chided me for the apology. "It's my preference," DeeDee countered. DeeDee became my friend, and in that harsh environment with its bleak hope, DeeDee learned about the beauty of words and spirit, and I learned about the brotherhood of the human soul.

Prison was not a good place for DeeDee. His discomforture was magnified by the unforgiving environment of prison and the secret anger that so many inmates hid. His trendy bouffant screamed loudly at the crude, hard men who had been locked up too long.

The whistles and catcalls did not hurt. The forcible rape by five hungry convicts did hurt. He fought savagely. They paid a heavy price for their bestiality. He was placed in solitary confinement for his own protection. The rapists were not even sanctioned. A month in solitary seems like a year. DeeDee was in solitary for six months before they decided to move him to another prison where he could get a new start. Perhaps things would be better for him there.

Things are never better for women trapped in men's bodies, who are forced to live among hard men with hard appetites. DeeDee retreated to his own cell. At least, they let him live alone. He spent hours cleaning it, arranging it, and adding imaginative touches of his own to the floor, the walls, and his bed.

He enrolled in an arts and crafts course and had access to yarn, needles, and patterns. A few touches of yarn to a T-shirt could make it almost pretty. Some embroidery added to a laundry bag could make a striking handbag for carrying all sorts of useful items.

He knitted ankle warmers that kept the harsh cold at bay. Sometimes he was almost pleased with his home, and even in this place, he found a few friends who respected him for who he was. He told them to call him DeeDee. He was tired of what he called the masculine charade.

I never could understand his preference, but I could understand his suffering. I still cannot understand why he chooses to be what he is, but I can understand midnight fear, and the pain of cruel rejection. DeeDee was my friend, and we shared the spirit of brotherhood.

To be black when all others are white –
To be wrong when all others are right—

To be poor when all others have wealth—
To be sick when all others have health—

To be blind when all others have sight –
To be weak when all others have might—

To be lame when all others can walk—
To be mute when all others can talk—

To have old when all others have new –
To be one when all others are two—

That's how it feels to be gay.

Tears on Young Cheeks

Jeff was nineteen years of age when he walked through the doors of a federal prison. He wore the mask of a tough street fighter, but his mask kept slipping and you could see the frightened boy hiding behind it. Besides, it's hard to present yourself as Hulk Hogan when you only weight 125 pounds. He had cut his hair in a military fashion to give the appearance of a formidable adversary, should some inmate wish to test him.

He talked a little too loudly. He cursed a little too much. His swagger was a little too pronounced for his slender frame. I knew he was scared to death. and who wouldn't be in a place like that? I weighed 210 pounds, but I never felt comfortable walking into a group of men whom I did not know. Sometimes that boy was terrified. I knew.

One Sunday afternoon I sat at a table in the common area of our pod. I watched Jeff enter and cross the room to the table next to mine. He sat alone with a writing pad and the stub of a pencil. He glanced at me several times and I think my presence helped him to relax even though the room was full of a menagerie of inmates.

He lost himself in the letter he was writing home. Occasionally, he asked me how to spell some particularly difficult word, but for the most part he ignored me and everyone else. He was thinking of his family.

And then the tears flowed down his young cheeks and dropped on his letter. His tough facade slipped to the floor, and he lost his pretense. He was just a boy again who was facing a sentence of twenty-five years for a crime he did not commit. The tears did not stop for a long time. I went back to my cell and cried too.

Several months later I was informed that I was being transferred to another prison. The night before my transfer I was stretched out on my bunk in my one-man cell. I heard a knock at the door and Jeff entered.

"Mr. Armsstrong, I just wanted to come and say good-bye to you. I hope you like your new place."

"Come in, Jeff. Sit down. I was sort of hoping I'd see you before I left."

He sat on my commode, the only seat available, and he lit up the room with his warm boyish smile. He was such a nice kid. I wondered if I would recognize him in fifteen or twenty years.

"Jeff, I don't want to embarrass you, but a couple of months ago I watched you writing a letter home and you were crying. I went back to my room and wrote a poem about you. I made an extra copy for you if you'd like to have it."

"Sure," he said.

"Let me read it to you." I unfolded the poem and slowly read it to him. When I finished, I looked up and saw he was crying and the tears flowed down his face, but he was not ashamed. I stood up to shake his hand and say good-bye, but a handshake was not enough. The boy in him needed a hug, and I hugged him.

I watched a suffering boy today
writing a letter home.
The room was full of his comrades,
but he was all alone.

Alone in his thoughts of a better day,
alone in his reverie.
His father, his mother, and brother there –
that place he longed to be.

The place where he grew to stature full,
and fun, as a boy was free.
Penalties were small and kindly dealt,
an ideal place to be.

An ideal place to be? Not here.
A prison's no haven of rest
Harsh times, hard men, and lonely nights,
the best of men will test.

I watched a suffering
man today.
Tears on his face were there.
Remorse, regret, and pain I know,
And his tears, I too, can share.

Part 3

How to Stay Alive

Prison is a dangerous place. Sure we have guards there, but they are there not so much to protect us as to protect them from us. Sometimes I have been more afraid of the guards than from the convicts.

When I first went in, I was somewhat oblivious to the prospect of danger. In reality there is often much more danger inside those walls than outside the walls. I have suffered through a few lock-downs and only then did I have more of a feeling of safety than the noise on the outside gave me.

After seven months in a medium-security facility I asked for and was moved to a Maximum prison. The first morning that I walked through the compound, a rather tough-looking young man came up to me and asked if I wanted to sell my new running shoes. I said that I didn't want to sell them.

He leaned towards me and silently said you better want to sell them, because I want them. I got the message loud and clear. He got the shoes and I got $15 dollars. He gave the money to me with a couple of guys watching. I figured it out.

I was assigned to a private cell In a unit that had once served as the Special Housing Unit for difficult prisoners. I noted that none of the doors were shut and locked at night. That didn't matter to me until I learned that the guy in the bunk next to me was a lifer. He had taken a couple of people out into the desert and killed them. He was not a very friendly person.

On my right was a man who, with his brother, were contract killers. All of us had open-door policies. I really wanted to get acquainted with both of them so I could write stories about them. It was not a good idea.

The title to this part of the book, **How to Stay Alive** does not imply that the intent is how to stay physically alive. The real meaning of this title refers how to stay alive mentally.

My father once said to me, "Son I don't want to die, but I sure don't want to die above the ears." The thing he feared most was not that his body would wear out, but that he would cease **to use his brain** by not thinking.

I know a lot of people who have died above the ears and meaningful conversation with them is useless. They have died above the ears.

I remember a man who claimed to have had 30 years of experience. Another man who knew him, said, "No, he has not had 30 years of experience. He has had one year of experience 30 times."

I am told that men do not read books. Women read nearly all of the books published. That statistic should open all of our minds to thinking why that is.

I thought it might be profitable to give you a list of some books that will keep your brain functioning. They have helped me. I think that they will help you.

A Beginning Reading List

John Steinbeck, ***The Grapes of Wrath***

Dale Carnegie, ***How to Win Friends
and Influence People***

S. I. Hayakawa, ***Language in Thought
and Action***

Napoleon Hill, ***Think and Grow Rich***

David Schwartz, ***The Magic of
Thinking Big***

Sam Shoemaker, ***Extraordinary Living
for Ordinary Men***

Visiting Day

The day that my parents visited me for the first time was a magnificent event. I met them in the visiting room. They were standing to greet me when I came in. I had never seen them smile so radiantly before.

Dad had left his overalls behind, and was dressed like he was going to church. Mom, in a brand new dress, never looked more beautiful. She kissed me full on the lips. Dad folded me into his arms and whispered in my ear, "Son, I love you."

We walked into the visiting yard. High walls were all around us, and on top of the walls, rolls of razor wire stretched endlessly. We found a bench and sat on it. We held hands. For two hours we talked. We laughed. We loved. Suddenly, my father was young again, and I could hear his words of more than 50 years before.

"If you go into the penitentiary, my love will crawl over the walls, go through the bars, and find you . . . Son, you will be loved every day you live."

The time together was too soon over. They had to leave. I had to return to my cell. Leaving the visiting room, I was strip-searched. All my clothes were removed and examined. My naked body was thoroughly inspected for contraband. They found nothing, of course.

Back in my seven-foot cell, I stretched out on the narrow cot to look at what my father had slipped me, and what the guards had failed to find when they searched me. Dad had passed me . . . my legacy.

In a flash, I saw how rich I really was—rich in all the things that matter. My father has just endowed me with a tremendous and valuable legacy—something that no one could take away from me."

I smiled, and lay back to luxuriate in my newfound wealth. The corners of my cell were no longer dark. My legacy had brightened the whole room. I had finally achieved real wealth.

Nine decades shaped that wrinkled brow.
Nine decades carved that back.

But it was God who made his heart;
'twas God who filled its lack.

Nine decades gnarled those country hands.
Nine decades bleached his hair.

His manners were simplicity.
No pretense! He wore no air.

Nine decades dimmed his honest eyes.
Nine decades choked his ears.

He held the Vision, resolute.
Faith conquered all his fears.

Now he stands a monument
to work that God can do.

From country boy of poverty,
to saint, and human, too.

The Indian's Victory

The prison bus headed north. Just one mile from the New Mexico border it turned off the freeway and headed for a large white building that looked very much like a mission. As we pulled to the front door, I saw coiled razor wire, stretching endlessly around the innocent-looking complex.

My cell was seven feet wide and eleven feet long. It included in that space, a john, a wash basin, and a cot for a second prisoner. A small window high on the wall had heavy wire over it. Even if one were successful in escaping through the window, there were rows of razor wire still to be penetrated. It was virtually escape-proof. This was my new home, sweet home.

The most interesting person in my unit was John, a giant Indian in his mid-fifties. His cell was next to mine but farther from the main entrance to our cells. This meant he had to pass my door several times a day.

He never looked in or acknowledged my presence. When I passed him in the narrow halls, he never said anything or even nodded. He never responded to a greeting. Bank robbery was his thing.

Weeks passed and John never took off the mask. There was never so much as a grunt in recognition of my presence. He was probably the most frightening of anyone I had met in prison, and I slept each night nervously. There was no locked door between us.

I studied John. I asked about him, but no one knew much, or would tell much. He stayed close to the other Indians, and it was obvious that he did not like white men. I knew he did not like me.

Months passed and never once did he utter a word to me, but I watched him pass my door. He wore his tribal bandana around his forehead. His long black hair fell down his back. His strong chin seemed to be stuck out in defiance to anyone in his way. He walked quietly, but he limped from an old bullet injury. It gave me the feeling that no bullet could stop this man, and I was afraid of him.

With no clear purpose, I started writing a poem about him. When it was finished I called it Red Man's Victory. I liked it. It seemed to describe him better than I could in prose.

One evening I went to his door, and in the friendliest tone I could muster, I said, "Hi, John. Could I come in for a minute?" He did not look up. He did not reply. I tried again. "John, I wrote a poem about you, and I'd like to come in and read it to you." He did not look up nor speak. It was as if I were not there at all. He said nothing, and continued what he was doing without even a pause.

"John, I'm going to read this poem to you. Now promise you won't hurt me if you don't like it. Okay?" He said nothing. I took another step into his room and sat down on the commode—the only place to sit in the small cell.

"I'm going to start now. Okay?" He still did not acknowledge my presence. Nervously, I started, "John, the title of my poem is Red Man's Victory."

He stands erect, with shoulders wide,
a man in form of God.
He has no home. He cannot hide
from punishment and rod.

His walls are high, his cell is dark,
the smell of freedom, weak.
And hope has died.
There is no spark, no holy grail to seek.

His face, long carved by cruel fate,
deep anguish, painted there.
Injustice etched hard lines of hate,
deep scars he's forced to bear.

As boy, he knew the simple things.
His friends were bird and bear.
His symphony all nature sings.
Innocence his robe to wear.

His youth, a shadow racing past.
Too soon his robe was torn.
Hard men, steel chains, claimed him at last.
Nobility and strength were shorn.

The red man walks a lonely trail
of history proud and free.
His victory cry, is now a wail
of bitter misery.

The Mother Lode

"Mr. Armstrong." It was Mrs. Lopez yelling at me across an expanse of floor that was being mopped. "Mr. Armstrong, get ready. You are going down to the camp. The warden approved it. Get ready. You're going." With that, she was off. It had only been three weeks since my request, and at that time, it was impossible. Now it was happening. I could hardly sleep that night.

The camp had no fences. There were few guards. It was a work camp, so everyone had a job. There were sheep to tend, fields to plow, and grounds to be kept neat. There was carpentry work, electrical work, plumbing, landscaping, and warehousing. I was made clerk of the chapel. No one asked me if I was a religious man. That didn't matter. It was a job they had to fill. This time they got it right. I thanked God.

By 6:30 each morning I was in the chapel. I entered silently, because I knew Billy would be there, praying.

He sat in his chair with a rosary in his hands and he prayed softy. He took cards from his pocket and slowly read the prayers printed on them. The cards looked as if they had been handled hundreds of times. I knew they had been. There was nothing more peaceful in my day than watching Billy pray.

A few minutes before seven, he put his rosary away. He stretched a rubber band around his cards and placed them in the pocket closest to his heart. He stood up and turned to me and greeted me. At the door he stopped and said, "God bless you," and very quietly he closed the chapel door and left for work. His words and spirit stayed in the chapel all day long.

I never had to prod myself to work, because I knew Billy was there praying for the warden, the inmates, and his family far away in Mexico. Sometimes he cried as he prayed. Sometimes I cried as I watched him. What a gentle soul he was! He couldn't have been more than 5'2", but he was strong. His hands showed that he had worked hard all his life. His gray hair and leathered face suggested he was in his late sixties. He had been in prison too long. I hoped he would go home soon.

"Not likely," a friend told me. "Billy will not be going home until he's served every day of his time. I doubt that he will make it to the end. He'll die here. They'll put him in the inmate's cemetery. He'll just be forgotten."

One afternoon, I noticed the camp administrator standing in the shade of the breeze-way between the administration building and the dining hall. He did not look busy, so I approached him.

"Mr. Woodward, can you tell me how I can do something I want to do and not get in trouble doing it?"

"Probably not. What do you want to do?"

"I hear there's a prison cemetery around here some place, and I want to go see it."

"What do you want to do that for?"

"I'm curious. I write stories, and I think there may be a story there."

"Come on. Let's go see," and with that he reached in his pocket for the key to his truck. We got in the truck and started down a narrow sandy lane—north. Then he turned east on a grassy trail, stopped, and pointed to a small, well-kept plot of land where neat markers stood in a row.

"There it is," he pointed. "You want to get out?"

"Sure," I said. "How many graves are there?"

"Last time I counted there were forty-nine."

We left the truck and walked out into the cemetery. Small brass markers were spaced neatly, and gave the names of the persons buried there, their birth dates, and the dates they died in prison. I guessed that Billy would be laid here. Perhaps he will be number fifty, I thought, and I could be number fifty-one.

We drove slowly back to the camp. That night I prayed for Billy and those whose bodies lay in the graves, and I prayed for myself.

Three birthdays spent I in this place,
a hell where hearts are cold;
where men in search of something warm,
dredge memories, rare as gold.

No guarantee for more than these,
the last could be this one.
And no one knows, and no one cares,
the glory that you've done.

Calendars can't tell your age,
when nights are century-long,
and days are weeks, and months are years,
and the mirror says, "the calendar's wrong."

What can you hold, and know for sure,
when your world is upside down?
Birthdays don't count. Each day is gold.
Now, the mother lode you've found.

Compassion's Garden

I saw him sitting on the bench outside receiving, wearing handcuffs. He did not look up when I passed. He glared at the floor, as if it was imperfect or unclean, and he was helpless to do anything about it. The expression on his face I had seen before. Was it bewilderment? Perhaps it was confusion or shock. I had seen it before and I knew it would pass.

Within a week he would laugh, and life would go on. If he had more hair, I thought, he could pass for Santa Claus. Perhaps he's in here for impersonation. You can get arrested for anything these days. Maybe he tore the tag off a mattress. Who Knows? Who cares?

A prison Camp is a work camp. It is not one of the prison country clubs that the media likes to create in the minds of the public. The reporters have never seen this place. Men work in the fields in August when the desert sun chases scorpions into their holes for relief. A passing January blizzard with cruel winds is no excuse for a day off. It wouldn't be so bad if inmates had gloves and warm coats, but here, it's every man for himself.

Everyone must work. There are no excuses. You can never get old enough to retire. Old men with tired backs shuffle their way to inane jobs. No malady is an excuse to be idle. Never mind spinal injuries, heart problems, diabetes, asthma, arthritis and a hundred other problems. This is a work camp. All men must work.

Ed Gibbon was assigned to the kitchen where he was made Emperor of the table tops. Three meals a day he had to wipe the tables after every inmate. The salt and pepper shakers had to be shined. It was not an easy assignment considering the fact that grease is the main staple of inmate diet. He began his day at five each morning, and at six that evening he was through for the day. He could go to his room between meals, but he was always on call. "Inmate Gibbon, report to the kitchen, NOW!"

The job was made more difficult by the fact that he couldn't get shoes to fit. He was issued someone's old worn shoes. They were the wrong size, and they hurt his feet. At night he soaked his feet in hot water to ease the pain and clean the blisters, but no one cared.

It was not long until the PCN (Prisoner's Communication Network) announced that the new inmate, Ed Gibbon, was a prisoner of conscience.

Conscience? That was shocking. I did not know there was a conscience in the whole institution, from the Warden on down.

The story was that he and a bunch of old geezers had the audacity to walk on U.S. Army grass and protest the operation of a school which trains foreign soldiers in the delicate arts of assassination, crushing protest, and controlling citizens. Unbelievable, I thought. I wonder what the true story is. That certainly can't be true.

"It's true," he said calmly. "I'm in here because a bunch of us have been protesting our government's running a school for assassins. Twenty-five of us are in prison because we refuse to stop our protest."

"What about the old geezer part?" I asked.

"That's just flattery. Actually we're a pretty diverse group. We have a Jesuit priest, a Methodist minister, a Maryknoll priest, a Unitarian minister, several nuns, a university professor, an artist, and a student. Our average age is fifty-eight. I guess that's where you get the geezer part.

There is simply too much poverty in this world. There is too much hate, and too much greed. Someone must do something about it, and I guess this is the garden where I have been placed to work."

I was struck by the fact that old geezers can still care, and can change evils by their compassion.

The seeds of greed sprout into war
and suck the blood of old and young.
The lights are gone. The hearth is cold,
and silence lives where hymns were sung.

And hungry eyes call out to him;
his heart moves toward the need.
His only gift is calloused hands;
he plants a garden. His tears are seeds.

The weeds and tares—they grow so fast
and choke the will of lesser soul.
He seeks not others' accolades—
compassion has its own rare goal.

He's not a giant, nor a saint.
His deeds have humble mien.
His heart's as big as the western sky—
He's God's gift to the poor unseen.

But, who will tend his garden when he's gone?

Cassandra

Cassandra Young was black, young, and pregnant. She dropped out of school to marry her sweetheart and have his baby. They were both sixteen years of age, but they were not afraid to work. For their first year of marriage they lived with her parents, and her mother took care of the baby girl while she worked. They named her Summer.

Their second year of marriage was more difficult, because her parents moved away and they had the extra expense of paying for an apartment and a baby-sitter. Some months they could not make ends meet. But it was the third year of marriage that did them in. Cassandra found herself pregnant again, and for a time, she could not work. The bills piled higher. The arguments came nightly.

"Cassandra, we've got to earn more money. We're getting in deep. Even working the second job we can't make it. We've got to have more money."

"Now Corey. We'll make it somehow."

"No we won't. Even if you work, by the time we pay for a baby-sitter, clothes, lunches, transportation, and taxes, there isn't anything left for the bills. We'll just get farther and farther behind. I don't have any choice. I've got to take that hauling job for Jo Jo."

"Now, we've both agreed that you won't do that. It's illegal."

"I've got to do something. We'll all starve if I don't. All I have to do is make one trip every weekend and I'll earn $500. In a little while I can pay all our bills and then I'll quit. There's nothing else I can do."

"But it's marijuana. You could go to jail."

"Cassandra, I won't smoke it. I'll just deliver it, and I'll be careful. It's only for a short time."

"If you do this, I'm going to go to mother's. I will not have anything to do with it. I don't want our two girls to grow up with a father in prison. I won"t have anything to do with it. I'll go to momma's."

"Well, maybe that's best. Jo Jo says I can live with him free. We'll save the apartment expense. We'll pay off our debts sooner this way."

"Corey, please don't do this. I'll work two jobs, too. We can hang on."

"If you go, I think I'll work with Jo Jo full time. I can make $1,500 a week that way. We'll be out of debt in four or five months. It's our only hope."

Cassandra took the children and went to her mother's. Corey called every week. Finally, he was getting old bills paid. He was making more money than he had ever dreamed possible. And he generously sent money to Cassandra and the children. He wrote her that in two more months they would be back together.

It never happened. He was arrested and charged with distribution. His court appointed lawyer said he would get twelve years.

The saddest part of the story was when the Federal Marshals came and arrested Cassandra for conspiracy. She knew, but didn't tell. That's a felony. At age nineteen she went to Carswell Federal Prison for women to serve a twenty-four-month sentence. Corey went to Three Rivers to begin a term of ten years. Their two daughters stayed with Cassandra's mother. I held my wife's hand as we sat in the visiting room. She had tears in her eyes as she told me the story of Cassandra.

"Honey, the saddest sight I've ever seen is when they pulled Cassandra's babies out of her arms because visiting hours were over. The babies were screaming to stay with their mother, and Cassandra just couldn't let loose of them. She was sobbing as badly as the children. And there was nothing I could do. I left with her, and when we got outside she nearly fell to pieces. I held her in my arms for a couple of hours while she cried her heart out. She's only nineteen herself and she has nearly two more years of suffering. As I see it, her biggest crime was that she was poor. Poverty is the cause of so much suffering.

Mr. Poverty cuts a mournful swath
through city, through town, and through dell.
He's careful to visit every home,
and offer his taste of hell.

Exempt—not one, of young or old;
they are his special delight.
And once they accept his sovereignty,
they seldom escape his might.

Mr. Poverty cares not for pain or woe.
Misery—his coin of exchange.
And always he walks, forever he stalks.
All men are within his range.

Curse him with voice. Defy him with deed.
Sad fruit is always his yield.
Flee if you like; he'll find you at last,
and plant you in Potter's Field.

Mother Without a Home

Cecil Cereceres was sentenced to sixty months under the conspiracy laws. There was no trial, only a plea agreement. The federal prosecutor had threatened to charge him with multiple counts, and Cecil could be sentenced to twenty years. Cecil's lawyer, a public defender, said it was wiser to accept five years, than take a chance on getting twenty years. This favorite tactic of prosecutors results in ninety-five percent of such cases being settled by plea. Less than five percent of these cases ever go to court. Poor people can't afford to go to court. They go to prison.

Cecil's prison was a citadel of flesh-tearing wire. He walked the halls there for three years. They were lonely years. Juanita, his wife, never visited once. She had no money. That's the way it is with poor people.

In the start of his fourth year Cecil was transferred to a work camp. Everyone had to work. Cecil was assigned to work at the sewage pond. He did not like the conditions, but the pay was good. By working seven days a week he could earn about $150 per month. Every month, he sent Juanita $140. It was the best he could do.

He read flow meters. He skimmed grease and debris out of lift stations. He sterilized sewage spills.

Some times the fumes were so bad that his asthma doubled him up with pain. There were other jobs. He could have asked for easier work, but the pay would be as low as $5 per month. Juanita needed the money. He had to keep his job.

Cecil had few friends at the camp. He worked ten hours each day. There were no holidays for him. He had no time for friends. He missed his family and the sermons of Father Berones.

He hoped the good father would understand that he was in prison because he could not violate his conscience. He was there because he would not testify against a friend who gave sanctuary to illegal aliens. Father Berones wrote him every week. The letters were his church.

The asthma attack came in the afternoon. The camp medic diagnosed it as an upset stomach. He ordered Cecil to take Maalox. Cecil struggled backed to his bunk, took the Maalox and lay down to rest. In the morning they found him dead in his bunk. He had bothered no one. It was his gentle way.

A fellow inmate wrote Juanita a letter. It was important for her to know the greatness of the man who was her husband. The children should know about this saint who was held in such a small body. Arizona would never again see a man of this character, never, perhaps in another hundred years.

Juanita sat at the kitchen table. She could cry no more. The funeral was in less than two hours. She sat and waited.

"Juanita?" Father Berones asked to be admitted. She nodded and he sat down at the table across from her in Cecil's chair. "Juanita, I have a letter for you. It is from a friend of Cecil's in prison. Do you want me to read it to you?"

She nodded her head, but looked out the window to the vine that wrapped itself around a trellis that Cecil had made. It gave them shade and beauty.

Father Berones tore open the envelope and began to read the words of condolence to the widow. As he read the careful words, he noticed she neither smiled nor frowned.

"Juanita," he begged. "Please listen to this last sentence. It's beautiful. Something broke inside him, but you must know his conscience did not break. They couldn't even bend it. Juanita, that is a great tribute."

She still did not smile nor did she frown. She took her eyes from the beautiful vine and looked at Father Berones. Quietly she said, "What am I supposed to do? Write that on the tombstone? Here lies a man with a conscience of steel. He left a mother without a home, and children without food."

She turned her eyes to the vine again, but did not cry.

A mother without a home and children without food.
Such was not in God's design.
He did not plan for created man
to build a garden so rude.

A mother without a home and children without food.
'Twas not in our founders' mind.
Their kindly words have lost their way
and selfishness is national mood.

A mother without a home and children without food .
It's our government's policy, today;
arrest the men and let them die
in prison's vast multitude.

I Cried Last Night

I am an army veteran of Word War II. Within weeks after the great explosions I stood at Nagasaki and Hiroshima and saw what terrible destruction man can create. I helped put Japan back together again. I had always felt great pride in my service to my country.

I was surprised to learn that even in prison there was a veteran's organization. The veterans met once every two weeks in the great hall upstairs in the administration building. I was introduced to a group of perhaps seventy-five veterans, as a World War II veteran.

There were only two of World War II types among the 1,300 inmates. Most were Nam vets. I could feel the camaraderie of the group. The sponsor asked us to stand. Two veterans marched to the front. One had a flag carefully folded in military fashion. Together, they unfolded the flag and held it before us.

The president of the association stood at attention and led us in the pledge of allegiance and in the singing of the national anthem. I was proud to participate in the ceremony, but I noticed that something was awry. I had never seen anything like this before.

Nearly one-half of the veterans had refused to salute the flag. They stood silently and gave no pledge of allegiance. They did not sing the national anthem. They stood immobile, like foreigners at an alien ceremony.

They stood at attention. Their jaws were locked. As if on command, they stared straight ahead. No eyes wavered. Their fists were clenched and held to their sides. These were military men all right, but to whose army did they belong? Something had gone wrong. For the time being, they coped as prisoners of war. The flag was refolded and the men placed it in its special cradle.

Stunned, I asked myself, Why were these veterans not participating in these simple acts of allegiance? Were these treasonous acts? No, I decided. These men felt that their country had committed treason against them, and now they were in a silent war against their own country.

That night in my bed I asked myself, how had such a condition come about? Why did these men feel the way they did?

When I was in the eighth grade my family moved to western Canada. It was a beautiful place, but now and then we got homesick. One day my father said to me, "Today, we are going to the States. We'll be back late tonight, but it will be fun." We drove to Sweetgrass, Montana and when we crossed the border we saw it—Old Glory was flying on top of a tall flagpole. Dad stopped the car and we got out. He took off his hat and put it over his heart, and I saw that he was crying. I cried, too, and I never forgot that picture.

The memory of Old Glory flying in the wind had been with me for many decades, and I wondered if the veterans that I saw that day had ever had an experience like that. The thought was sad enough to cry over.

I cried last night. I don't know why.
There were no tears;
my cheeks were dry.

But deep inside, a memory
escaped its grave
to capture me.

Long hidden deep, it rose again
to vex my soul—
to bare my sin.

Today I muse, and wonder why
dead memories
can make me cry.

So many things I do not know,
when night's a battle,
the past—a foe.

But when I see the sun again,
I think perhaps
this day, I'll win.

Prisoners All

By the time I was located in my third institution, I was adjusted to how things operate in the federal system. The problem was, however, that the inmates and staff were always different, and if you did not know and understand them, you could have a hard time. Sometimes there was an informal inmate system that ran things, while the staff mostly left their hands off if things were running smoothly. They didn't get involved in a lot of mundane activities, although these activities were important to the inmates. That's the way it was at my third institution.

Gater Bumpus was the informal commander of our camp. He was sixty years old, six foot seven inches tall and a hulk of muscles. He had spent most of his years in prisons of one kind or another. He was initiated into the system while just a teenager. There were periods when he was on the outside, but they were of short duration. Somehow, he quickly found his way back to familiar surroundings. He had dabbled in theft of various kinds, drugs, safecracking, robbery, and other forms of crime which the law knew nothing about. He knew that some inmate ran nearly every prison, and he elected himself to that position, and even the authorities accepted that as his rightful position. He was useful to inmates and guards alike. If you wanted anything done, you went to Gater. Of course, it would cost you, but it was always worth it.

One of my jobs as clerk of the chapel was to distribute Christmas cards to every inmate at Christmas time. Hallmark and other card companies donated thousands of Christmas cards to every prison, and the prison gave them to the inmates. Some of the cards were very expense and beautiful. Some were quite ordinary, but they were free and each inmate usually received about a dozen cards to send out to a wife, parents, relatives or friends.

When it came time to distribute the cards, I asked a few friends to help me distributed them. What I did not know was that Gater usually controlled the distribution of these cards. He gave the good ones to his close friends, and the small and unattractive cards went to the new comers and the inmates who were out of favor with Gater.

When Gater found out that I had distributed them without his permission, he put a hex on me. He would not talk to me nor recognize me. The word was out that I was cursed, and all should leave me alone. And, they did. For months I was frozen out and Gater made my life miserable whenever he could.

When I was informed about my infraction, I went to Gater and asked for forgiveness. I was placed on his probation, but eventually I was released. I learned a lot from Gater over the months that followed. Later, when we were released, he called me often, sometimes every week. I called him, too.

But one day the telephone numbers that he gave me became inoperable. They said the numbers were no longer active. Something had happened. Perhaps, he violated the terms of his release, and they put him back inside. Perhaps he died from his numerous ailments. I do not know, but I miss him. We were comrades under arms, for a while, and after all he was a prisoner and I was a prisoner, too. On reflection, it seems to me that most of the people that I know are prisoners of something. Real freedom is a scarce commodity, and to get it, one must start with the heart and its fickle attitudes. It's time for more people to be released, and to live in freedom.

They say I don't look like a prisoner,
but they can't see the chains I hide.
They say my smile is a signal light,
that things are okay, my life's all right.

They say I don't act like a prisoner.
My step is too jaunty, my bearing too light.
They don't see that my road is a rocky one,
when I travel the shadows, where faith is undone.

They don't listen at night when the halls are still,
when the noise is gone, and silence rings loud.
They don't see those midnights, where I must fight
the bad that I've done, and so little right.

They look for my scars. They see not a one.
They don't know the savage of being alone.
No ugly tattoos, put painfully there,
nor gasp at the wounds that I silently bear.

All men are prisoners of deed or of fame,
and all men scream at their pain.
Prisoners all, keep a pleasant facade,
but our ashes and anguish we show only to God.

Happiness Has a Fickle Soul

Jerry was a student in one of the GED classes that I tutored. He was nearly forty years old, but he had dropped out of high school his first year, and he never saw a reason to return. I liked him. He was bright and had a great wit. We became good friends.

"Come up to my room. I want to show you something." Jerry was temporarily housed by himself, and he had made a display on his small table that looked almost like a shrine.

"This is my wife," he said pointing to a photograph of a beautiful woman posing in a glamorized setting. "And these are my two kids."

"She's lovely! What beautiful kids!" I said.

He grinned at the compliment. "Yeah, but I won't be able to keep them. She's only 26 and I'm 40. When I get out, I'll be 50. I can't expect her to wait for me. She's too young and beautiful, and she deserves some happiness in life. I know I'll lose her. Her name's Florine."

"Does she ever visit you?" I asked.

"Oh, now and then, but I can see—she's leaving. I don't blame her. I am a little angry that she's spent my money on some guy who doesn't love her like I do. I left her in good financial shape, but she's blowing it. It kinda drives me crazy sometimes. She's even quit sending me cigarette money. I guess I have to admit —it's over."

Jerry Franklin sat at the table where an important card game was going on. It was Sunday afternoon, and this card game would go on into the night. Jerry was down $150, and I wondered how he would pay the boys. It was dangerous not to pay some of them.

Jerry rose between hands, stretched, and said, "Be back in a minute." He walked to his room, just steps away, went in, and shut the door. The boys in the game separated to gather snacks. They returned, refreshed and ready to win some more money.

"Jerry, come on, we're ready" one of them called out.

"Jerry, hurry up," Big George yelled. Big George pushed back his chair, rose, and walked to Jerry's door. "Jerry!" Big George took the knob, opened the door, and started to enter, but two legs dangled directly in front of him. Jerry had hanged himself with a sheet. As they laid his body on the floor, a guard tried to revive him, but it was too late.

That night in the dark, I cried.

Who would tell Florine? I wondered, Would she ever find happiness?

Happiness is not a goal
that any one should seek.
the price of it is far too dear;
it robs the high and meek.

But search for treasure deeply hid.
Mind not the toil or tears.
Turn not aside to idle joy—
mind not your midnight fears.

For life will yield what 'er you seek.
glib transience lasts a day.
True value lasts a million years.
Rewards are there to stay.

Happiness will come and go—
it has a fickle soul.
But good and right go on and on.
Make them your daily goal.

And when you reach the end of day
and count all that you bless,
Because you sought the good and right,
you now have … happiness.

Mail Call

The two most important things to those inside, are a visit on visiting day, and a letter from someone who cares about them. I met several inmates who had never had a visit, nor had a letter in all the years they were in prison. Nevertheless, they nearly always showed up when mail call was announced. Their needs for contact surmounted the disappointments of not receiving anything, day after day.

My wife and I both made a pledge to each other that we would write every single day, seven days a week. She often wrote me more than one letter a day. We were true to our pledges for the years that we were apart. Perhaps, that is why we are now together. There is nothing that you can do that is more important than to visit or write a person whom you care about and who is inside.

We both went into prison on January the third. One year passed, and on New Year's Day, she wrote me a letter that I cherish to this day. I share it with you.

Happy New Year

1. I've learned that nothing can separate me from the love of God.

2. I've learned that nothing can separate me from your love.

3. I've learned that nothing can separate me from the presence of God.

4. I've learned that nothing can separate me from your presence.

5. I've learned that all of the principles of godly living work. I've learned that they work particularly well in the bad situations of life.

6. I've grown to love some very special little girls, who I never would have known and loved, if I had not gone to prison.

7. I've learned that most of the people in prison are not bad people. They are people who have done bad things, and made some bad mistakes, but most of them are not bad.

8. I've learned that even when people are acting bad, they may not be bad. Most people struggle to be good and do good. It's just that we all fall short.

9. I've learned that there is no them and us. We are all God's people, created by Him. He loves us all with our pimples, scars, and shortcomings. I've consistently rejected the "these people" attitude and can say I like and love the staff, officers, and all—with the same heart that I love the inmates.

10. I've discovered that there are many good, caring people within the Bureau of Prisons—more good and caring than not. For this I am thankful.

11. I've discovered that our love can endure separation, and grow stronger through it.

12. I've discovered that the attributes of God (the fruit of the Spirit) are actually spiritual forces with tremendous power. That is one of the best things I've discovered. This is a "pearl of great price."

13. I've discovered, once again, how blessed I am to have lived for so many years with a man of God who has the gift of wisdom. You have showered me with the fruit of the spirit of God. I am so blessed.

14. I've discovered that material things (while they pull at your flesh) do not matter. It is the spiritual things that matter. You are one of the spiritual things that I am referring to. You matter! Family matters! Not much else matters unless it enhances the things that do matter. That is another pearl of great price.

15. I've discovered that God will use the yielded heart wherever it is—in prison or out of prison. It does

not matter where you are. The whole world is His, and everything in it. That includes both of our prisons. They belong to Him, and he will call and use His children in these places.

16. I've discovered that I cannot always control what happens to me, but I can control what happens in me. Another pearl.

17. I've discovered that Philippians 4:8 not only works. It's powerful!
"Whatsoever things are true, whatsoever things are honest, whatsoever things area just, whatsoever things are pure, whatsoever things are lovely, whatsoever things are of good report; if there be any virtue, if there be any praise, think on these things."

18. I've discovered that what you told me before we came to prison is true. You said, "Sherry, I've discovered whenever I go through a problem in life, I am better off when I get to the other side of it." I am not even to the other side, but I can already see that it is true.

19. I've discovered that of ten fears walking down the road at me, nine of them are going to fall in the ditch before they ever get to me.

20. I've discovered that I love you more today than before. (I didn't think that was possible).

21. I've discovered that our life is not fluff. It's made of good stuff, which can go through the bad

times.

22. I've discovered that the benefits of being in prison have outweighed the negatives. How can that be? It must be Jesus.

23. I always knew I was the most blessed woman and the richest in the world. Now, I know it with new vigor. No one can take that away from me.

24. I've discovered that happiness is having you and having Jesus. I always knew it, but this year it stood the test. I am thankful for the test.

25. I've discovered that I have everything I need in this world to be happy. It is my choice whether or not I live in it.

These are a few of the things I am thankful for. My heart is abundantly full, and I am happy this New Year's Day. We will have a wonderful new year, because we will make the right choices. God abundantly provides for us—our part is in the choosing.

Sherry

I Love Adventure

Since this book has been offered as a **case study,** please go with me through some highlights of my journey. Every step of my journey has been a great adventure.

My boyhood was a great adventure and I loved every minute of it. I played *cops and robbers, cowboys and indians* and *Yanks and Nazis.* My heroism in all of the battles struck fear in the heart of my best friend, Dean Wilmoth. Some 80 years later we still have our skirmishes, but mosty we just sit and reminisce. Of course, we were both wounded many times and we still have the scars to remind us of the battles of our youth.

But youth passes quickly, and before we know it we are in those reality years. When I was just 18 years of age I was drafted into the US Army. Basic training was short because I was in a unit scheduled to go to the Battle of the Bulge. But the war in Europe ended abruptly and my unit was re-routed to Japan. I was one of the first US soldiers to experience the devastation of the atomic bombs in both Nagasaki and Hiroshima. I didn't feel 18 any longer. The fun and games of youth were gone.

I was in my mid-twenties when war again knocked on the door of America. At that time the papers were full of the stories of three young men in Cuba who were leading a revolution against the Batista dictatorship in Cuba. Fidel Castrp, his brother Raul, and Che Guevara were the Robin Hoods of my era and they had guns—not arrows. I went to Cuba to see Havana, but Castro's Machine gun fire from a passing car chased me to find a more secure place. I went home.

In the mid 1950s, desegregation was the hot issue. I decided to attempt to enroll in an all-black university to see if a white student would get the same reaction in a black University as a black student would get in an all-white University. I chose Atlanta University, a prestigious black institution, to try my experiment. Amazingly, I got in and became the first white student to explore the reverse reality of prejudice. That experience was a battle of a different kind.

During the 1960s the Congo massacres were in the headlines of the world's newspapers. I decided to go see the carnage myself. The trip into the Congo was uneventful, but, on the way out I ran into a guerilla action and barely escaped with my life.

One of the highlights of living in Africa was a visit that I took to a leper colony in Swaziland. I toured the small leper village as a guest of the director of the colony. The picture of dozens of natives who had been tortured by leprosy is seared on my brain forever. Luncheon served to me by lepers was not one of my most enjoyable dining experiences.

I was in Saigon in the early days of that dreadful war. I went as a civilian—not as a soldier. I wanted to see if it was as bad as the newspapers said it was. The slit trenches near the sidewalks announced that you could expect an enemy plane to bomb or strafe the area at any time. I didn't get straifed but I narrowly missed the bombing of the Army Officer's hotel next door.

In South America I visited the site where seven American missionaries were killed on the shores of the Amazon river by native head-hunters. In Ecuador. a side trip lead to hunting alligators at midnight. A couple of missionaries assured me that it was completely safe and it was. We caught three alligators, and ignored the thousands of piranha.

The Six-Day-War between Israel and Egypt is one of History's great events. I decided to see it for myself and visited Israel the week after the war was over. I decided to go down the road to Jericho. I didn't see a single good samaritan, but I did see a couple of Israeli tanks still smoldering on the battlefield. I avoided a rocket attack at the Sea of Galilee one late night. I love adventure.

I will never forget visiting the upper regions of Mozambique where lions and mambas are a constant threat. Natives live in constant fear of their lives in that harsh environment.

On the road to Victoria Falls in old Rhodesia, a student and I were attacked by three giant bull elephants. Our small volkswagon sputtered slowly away from the danger.

I guess you could call me an adventurer. . . . . with an occasional cowardly bent.

Addendum

I cannot count the number of requests that have come to me for a copy of a particular poem or story that I have written. I cannot remember all the promises that I gave to inmates, that I would not forget them—that I would send them a copy of my poems and stories as soon as they become available. The words of these inmates are still vivid in my memory.

"...my wife really needs to read that poem. She never has understood how the system works."

"...I need to get those stories and poems to my children. They are old enough to understand the prison problem."

"...I wish my church could read all your stuff. I think it would be more compassionate to inmates and to their families."

"...every inmate needs to read that stuff. You don't have to waste your time while you are in here. Your stories prove that."

Currently, there are over 2,000,000 inmates in these prisons. Perhaps we can help some of them grasp a new idea and a new spirit.

Thank you for your compassion.

A Personal Note

If you have read this far into this book, I know you, too, have seen the great pain of prison. You have also seen the possible promise that can come from incarceration.

I Have a Dream

II would like to get copies of this book out to where it will do the most good. To jails, to prisons, to churches to families who have children in prison. Each book can be delivered for $4 each.

5 books to a local jail..............$20

10 books to a prison...............$40

20 books to a church ....,$80

Any amount can be delivered for $4 each

Send your check to:

Dr. Kenneth Armstrong

Books

Fort Towson, OK 74735

(If you would like to deliver the books yourself, just indicate how many you want and send a check to cover the $4 for each book.)

In His Own Words

My name is Kenneth Shelby Armstrong. I didn't come along until 1927, but my parents chose an auspicious place for my birth. They chose Skedee, Oklahoma.

From the outset I knew that I was special. Not many people can say that they were born in Skedee. The exclusivity of my place of birth has permitted me to hold my head high on all occasions.

At one time I was Bud Wilkinson's guest when he had an office in the White House. Even on that occasion, I felt that special pride of knowing that probably not one other person in the entire place had been privileged to having been born in Skedee. For those of us who are culturally aware, being born in Oklahoma is a secret form of royalty.

I started out to be an educator and a minister, but somewhere along the way I caught a detour that led me in a new direction. Following that uncertain journey, I discovered a new occupation—writing. Today, I sit at my computer, look across a beautiful lake, and I write.

I have traveled the world. I have lived in Japan, South Africa and Canada. I have visited more than 60 countries of the world, but there is no place like home. Now I live in Fort Towson, Oklahoma on a small lake

—Lake Raymond Gary. Fort Towson is a bigger place than Skedee, but not by much. It is a democracy of gracious common people with whom I am honored to live in community.

Education

U. of N.M. (M.A. in Philosophy)

N.T.S. (B.D. in Theology)

U. of Kansas (Doc. Studies, Human Relations.)

U. of Denver (Ed.D., in Higher Ed.)

Iliff at Denver U. (Th.D., in Sociology of Rel.)

Atlanta U. (Social Work)

Books by

Kenneth Shelby Armstrong

— — —

My Very Best Stories

A regular feature published weekly in *The Hugo Daily News* is a column entitled, *In His Own Words.* This column consists of the short stories of Dr. Armstrong. These stories were so inspiring that the Editor suggested that they be put in book form. Readers of all ages will enjoy them.

Available at: www.Amazon.com Go to: Books and enter Kenneth Shelby Armstrong and the title of this book.

— — —

Will it Be Dangerous?

Will it be dangerous? Could I get killed? These two question plagued Dr. Armstrong as he enrolled in an all-black university as the only white student in the entire school. Murder was not the outcome but it was no romp. He received the kind of treatment at Atlanta University that black students received at Mississippi, Alabama, Texas and other southern universities. Later he went to Africa and taught at an all-white college and no blacks were allowed. You will be amazed as you read his other adventures.

Available at: www.Amazon.com Go to: Books and enter Kenneth Shelby Armstrong and the title of this book.

— — —

What Ever Happened to Robin?

On the sandy shores of Lake Biwa in Japan, a distinguished American bishop lays his head in the lap of a beautiful Japanese woman and dies. His death reveals a secret that he had held since he was a young soldier in Kyoto during the World War II American occupation of Japan. This is a historical romance that must be read.

Available at: www.Amazon.com Go to: Books and enter Kenneth Shelby Armstrong and the title of this book.

— — —

How to Strive, Thrive and Stay Alive in Prison

Staying alive in prison is not an easy task. This year more than 2,000,000 men and women will go behind bars and fight for safety, meaning, and a bleak future. Some, on the other hand have found secrets to making the experience profitable. The stories told here will make you **fear** and in some cases **cheer**.

Available at: www.Amazon.com Go to: Books and enter Kenneth Shelby Armstrong and the title of this book.

— — —